Get CONNECTED to DIGITAL LITERACY

Great GAME DESIGN

Clive Gifford

Crabtree Publishing Company

www.crabtreebooks.com

Crabtree Publishing Company
www.crabtreebooks.com
1-800-387-7650

Published in Canada
Crabtree Publishing
616 Welland Ave.
St. Catharines, ON
L2M 5V6

Published in the United States
Crabtree Publishing
PMB 59051, 350 Fifth Ave.
59th Floor,
New York, NY

Published in 2018 by CRABTREE PUBLISHING COMPANY.

First published in 2017 by Wayland
(A division of Hachette Children's Books)
Copyright © Hodder & Stoughton 2017

Author: Clive Gifford
Project editor: Sonya Newland
Designer: Rocket Design (East Anglia) Ltd
Editors: Sonya Newland, Kathy Middleton
Proofreader: Petrice Custance
Prepress technician: Ken Wright
Print and production coordinator: Margaret Amy Salter

Consultant: Lee Martin, B. Ed, E-Learning Specialist

Printed in the USA/072017/CG20170524

Photographs:
All images courtesy of Shutterstock except:
Alamy: p.13b (Reuters), p.16 (Ian Dagnall),
p.18b (Reuters); iStock: p.9br (LICreate), p.10b
(klerik78), p.15b (ilbusca), p.18t (PandaWild),
p.27b (Maxiphoto); Wikimedia: p.7t (Pargon),
p.27t (Jordifferer).

While every attempt has been made to clear copyright, should there be any inadvertent omission this will be rectified in future editions.

Disclaimer: The website addresses (URLs) included in this book were valid at the time of going to press. However, because of the nature of the Internet, it is possible that some addresses may have changed, or sites may have changed or closed down since publication. While the author and publisher regret any inconvenience this may cause the readers, no responsibility for any such changes can be accepted by either the author or the publisher.

Note to reader: Words highlighted in bold appear in the Glossary on page 30. Answers to activities are on page 31.

Library and Archives Canada Cataloguing in Publication

Gifford, Clive, author
  Great game design / Clive Gifford.

(Get connected to digital literacy)
Includes index.
Issued in print and electronic formats.
ISBN 978-0-7787-3622-6 (hardcover).--
ISBN 978-0-7787-3633-2 (softcover).--
ISBN 978-1-4271-1958-2 (HTML)

  1. Computer games--Programming--Juvenile literature.
2. Computer games--Design--Juvenile literature. I. Title.

QA76.76.C672G54 2017   j794.8'1526   C2017-903181-3
                                                   C2017-903182-1

Library of Congress Cataloging-in-Publication Data

CIP available at the Library of Congress

Contents

Fun on the Screen

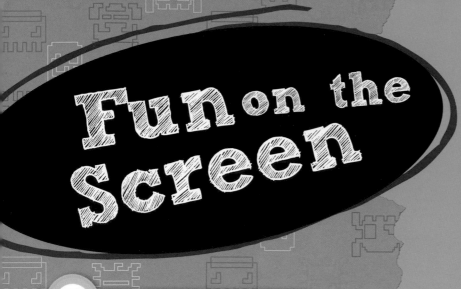

Computer games (also known as video games) are a type of computer program. They are made up of lines of code, which are instructions to the computer, arcade machine, or game **console**. Games were once played only in black and white on large, silent computers in businesses and colleges. Today, they blaze with color and action, roar with sound, and are played everywhere!

Big business

Computer gaming is now a major industry. There are more than 3,000 computer-game companies just in North America. New games are launched with a splash of publicity, just like major movies. It is big business: computer game sales worldwide were $91 billion US in 2015.

COMPUTER Hero!

Most computer games today are the work of a large team of people. In 2009, the first version of Minecraft was created and coded by just one person, Markus Persson (also known as Notch), from Sweden. Persson wrote his first simple computer game at the age of eight!

Markus Persson

Games everywhere

Games can be played on personal computers, laptops, and tablets. They can also be played on smartphones or handheld game consoles for users on the move. When a game is created, it is often converted to different formats so it can work on many different machines. This is called **porting**.

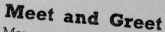

Tetris was invented in 1984.

TRUE STORY

Out of this World! The first video game played in space was Tetris. Invented in 1984, the goal of the game is to fit falling blocks together like a puzzle. In 1993, it was played by Russian cosmonaut Aleksandr Serebrov on a Nintendo Game Boy (a handheld game machine) on the MIR space station.

Meet and Greet

Many game players, or gamers, compete against one another in game competitions. Gamers and game makers meet at events called conventions. The world's biggest gaming convention is Gamescom, which is held in Cologne, Germany, each year. In 2016, 345,000 people attended!

Early Computer Games

Electronic computers were first built and used in the 1940s, during World War II. These early machines were used for work that was deadly serious, such as doing math to predict where a shot from a cannon would fly. But it wasn't long before some programmers started having a little fun...

The first game

In 1950, Bertie the Brain was demonstrated in Canada. This computer was 13 feet (4 meters) tall and could play against a human at Tic-Tac-Toe. Early games included checkers and simple chess programs. Usually, only scientists or students got to play them because computers were rare and expensive at that time. Most were used by the military, government departments, or universities.

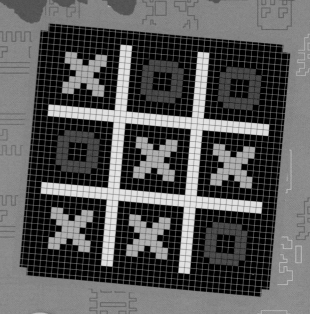

Spacewar!
Spacewar! was the first computer action game. The code was developed by an American college student, named Steve Russell, and his friends. It was first played in 1962 and featured two spaceships battling each other on a PDP-1 computer's small, round screen. This type of game later became known as an arcade game.

Gaming boom

Computer games boomed in the late 1970s and 1980s. More and more people had gained access to computers. Handheld game machines were also becoming popular. As computers became more powerful, creators were able to make games that were more colorful and detailed.

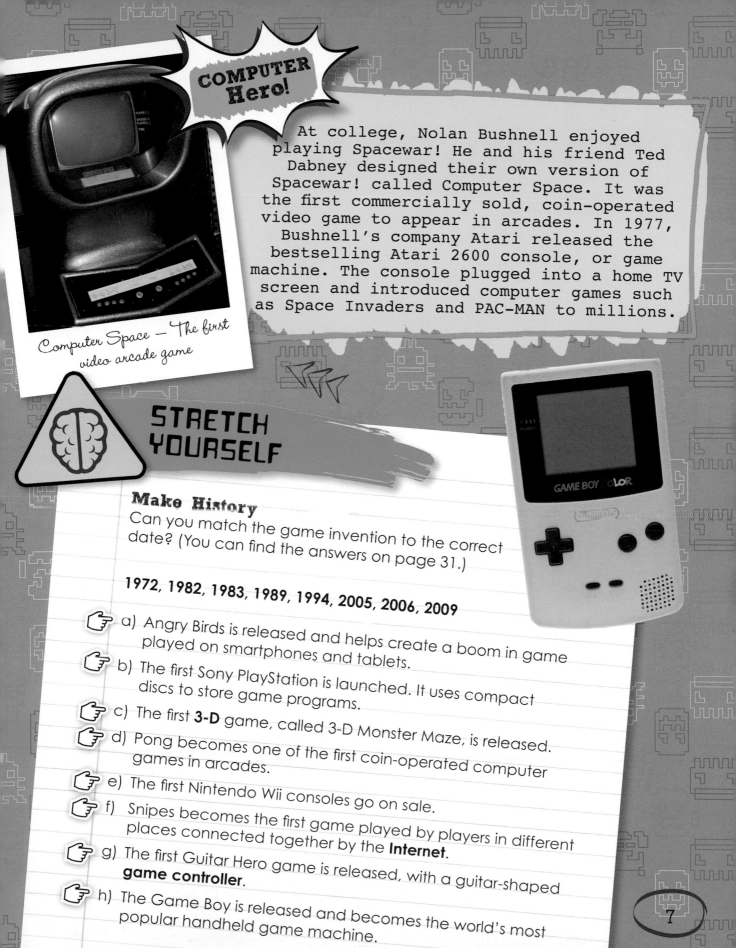

COMPUTER Hero!

At college, Nolan Bushnell enjoyed playing Spacewar! He and his friend Ted Dabney designed their own version of Spacewar! called Computer Space. It was the first commercially sold, coin-operated video game to appear in arcades. In 1977, Bushnell's company Atari released the bestselling Atari 2600 console, or game machine. The console plugged into a home TV screen and introduced computer games such as Space Invaders and PAC-MAN to millions.

Computer Space — The first video arcade game

STRETCH YOURSELF

Make History

Can you match the game invention to the correct date? (You can find the answers on page 31.)

1972, 1982, 1983, 1989, 1994, 2005, 2006, 2009

a) Angry Birds is released and helps create a boom in game played on smartphones and tablets.

b) The first Sony PlayStation is launched. It uses compact discs to store game programs.

c) The first **3-D** game, called 3-D Monster Maze, is released.

d) Pong becomes one of the first coin-operated computer games in arcades.

e) The first Nintendo Wii consoles go on sale.

f) Snipes becomes the first game played by players in different places connected together by the **Internet**.

g) The first Guitar Hero game is released, with a guitar-shaped **game controller**.

h) The Game Boy is released and becomes the world's most popular handheld game machine.

Types of Games

There are many genres, or types, of games. Here are some of the most popular genres.

 Traditional and puzzle games

These include card games such as solitaire and snap, puzzle games such as Candy Crush Saga, and board games such as chess and checkers. In many of these games, the computer acts as the opponent against the human player.

Sports and racing

From FIFA 17 and NBA Live to Wii Sports Resort, many games allow people to play a computer version of a sport. Racing games let gamers race cars, motorbikes, skateboards, and many other vehicles on tracks or through digital scenes.

Shooters

The popular genre of shooting game includes classics such as Defender and games for adults such as Call of Duty and Halo. Some show the action from above. Others are first-person shooters (FPS). These games display the action as if looking through the character's eyes.

Platform games

Characters in these games have to jump, duck, run, and swing to move between platforms, pass obstacles, and overcome enemies to travel through the game's levels. Super Mario 64, Tomb Raider, and the Rayman series are popular platform games.

Adventure and sandbox games

In adventure games, players follow a story, meet other characters, and solve puzzles to complete a quest or task. Sandbox games, such as Minecraft, also have a world to explore. These games are open-ended, which means there is more than one way to complete the game.

Minecraft

Simulations

Simulation games mimic a real-life situation, such as owning a pet or flying an aircraft. Some, such as SimCity, give players the task of building a town or, such as Madden NFL, players run an American Football team.

Rhythm games

Games such as Guitar Hero and Just Dance challenge a player's timing and sense of rhythm. Players have to match on-screen moves to dance or play tunes, sometimes as part of a group.

9

Storyboards

The action and the sequence, or order, of events in a game have to be carefully planned and mapped out. One way to do this is to create **storyboards**, which act as a visual script or plan of the game's action.

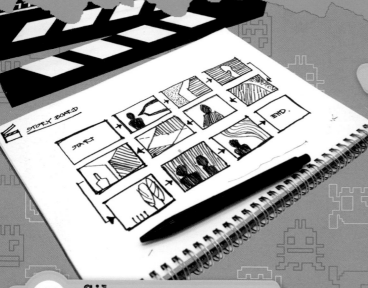

Finding your way

Storyboards allow game designers to move scenes or different parts of action around to get the order and story correct before they begin writing the code. Some game makers use storyboards as a way of judging how the gameplay might work on a particular level or part of their game. For example, on a platform or maze game, they may sketch out all the different routes through a level to help them judge whether they are too easy or difficult.

Silver-screen storyboarding

Storyboarding was first developed by the makers of cartoons and animated movies. Walt Disney and his team often used this technique a lot from the 1930s onward. Later, makers of movies with live actors also began storyboarding. Directors would use sketches of each scene to determine how to position lighting and cameras. They also used sketches to show the cast and crew how the film's scenes would look and how the story would progress.

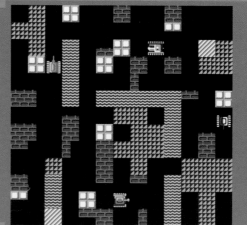

Many computer games feature **cutscenes**. The action in a cutscene may slightly further the game's story, show characters talking to one another, or give the player clues or tips. Lengthy, detailed cutscenes for major games are storyboarded just like the game action. PAC-MAN and Space Invaders II were among the first major games to feature cutscenes.

STRETCH YOURSELF

Your Own Storyboard

To get an idea of how storyboarding works, grab some large sheets of paper and draw four, six, or eight equal-sized rectangles on each page. These are your blank storyboards. Pick a fairy tale, fable, or another short story you have read, and try to tell the story in up to 16 separate storyboard entries.

You can use arrows on the scenes to show movement and write short notes underneath each image. Don't worry if you're not the world's best artist. Just sketch in each scene to tell the story. Think about the following:

☞ How will you set the scene at the start?

☞ How will the characters or objects move around?

☞ If there are different scenes, how will you move between them?

☞ Will there be jokes or a surprise ending?

☞ What sort of cutscene would you show to celebrate when a player has completed a game or a level successfully?

Game Assets

All the things viewed in a computer game, such as characters, vehicles, obstacles, tools, and weapons, are called **assets**. Artists design them, and then assets are turned into digital form by graphic designers who create computer models. Coders write the instructions to make the models work, move, and react in the game.

 ## Early game art

The first computer action games, such as Computer Space and Pong, were black and white because early screens could not show color. Color games arrived in the 1970s, but assets still did not look very sophisticated. Screens could only show low numbers of **pixels**, which are dots that combine to make an image on the screen. The number of pixels a screen can display is called its resolution. As computers increased in power and resolution, graphics improved dramatically.

TRUE STORY

Bad Memory? Game in the past had to be coded to run on small amounts of computer **memory**. The smash hit platform game Super Mario Bros. occupied just 31 kilobytes (KB) of memory. A modern game can be a million times that size!

Gamers try out an old-fashioned game on a black-and-white screen.

Game artists illustrate the different assets in a game, from scenery to weapons. Important game characters usually get the most attention and can take a game artist weeks to get right. Everything that a player interacts with in a game is designed with great care.

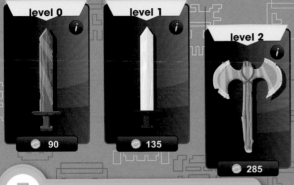

SOUND, SPEECH, AND MUSIC

The sounds and speech that occur in a game are also assets. Just like graphics, these assets have to be planned and produced. Modern games have a lot of dialogue. For example, the action role-playing game Fallout 4 contains more than 111,000 spoken lines. These all have to be recorded by voice actors.

3-D assets

Many modern games are three-dimensional. This means the game's assets have to be turned into 3-D models that can be viewed from any angle. 3-D modeling usually requires building a skeleton or outline of the asset. Hinges (also known as hinge points or **avars**) are added to these models. Hinges allow programmers to write code that will alter these points to move parts of the object during the game. The outer surface, or covering, of the asset is added using programs that create the look of different textures. The programs can mimic all sorts of materials to cover it.

Motion capture

One way of creating a 3-D computer model is by using motion capture. Human actors wear a special suit, often fitted with strips or balls. These added pieces mark the points of movement on the actor's body as he or she is filmed. Their movements are translated into computer data, which is then applied to a 3-D model of a character in the game. Motion capture is often used in sports simulations and fighting games to create realistic-looking movement.

Game Characters

Most games feature characters of some kind, and a lot of thought goes into the characters for a major game. Teams of artists make hundreds of sketches before they hit upon the right design.

 Big impact

Characters are the stars in their game. Some have become so popular, they are considered gaming icons. These include PAC-MAN, Red (below) from the Angry Birds game, and Mario, the plumber with a moustache. He first appeared in 1981 in the game Donkey Kong. Gamers loved him! Mario has appeared in more than 200 games, and starred in a movie and TV show!

 Cast of characters

In most games, the user plays a particular character. However, there is usually a wide range of other characters, too. Non-player characters, or NPCs, are controlled by the computer. Some NPCs may be allies or friends of the main game character. Others are opponents that a player's character must avoid or defeat in order to progress in the game.

Bosses

Bosses are characters that are found near the end of a level in many games. They are harder to defeat than other opponents. A boss represents the biggest challenge before a gamer can move on to the next level. One famous boss is Bowser (right), who is found in many Mario and Super Mario games.

STRETCH YOURSELF

Create a Character!

Grab some paper and design three characters of your own for a computer game: a hero or heroine (the gamer's character), a bad guy who gets in the way or chases the hero or heroine, and a boss who must be confronted at the end of the game. Ask yourself these questions:

☞ What special abilities do you want each character to have?

☞ How would the character stand out against the game background?

☞ What clothing would they wear?

☞ What accessories or tools would they carry?

☞ How would players use each character in the game?

☞ What strengths and weaknesses would each character have?

TRUE STORY

A Slice of History. The famous PAC-MAN character was invented by the Japanese game designer Toru Iwatani while he was eating his dinner! He was inspired by the shape of a pizza with a slice removed.

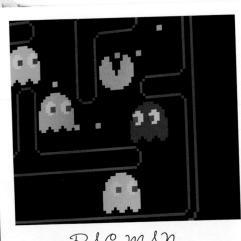

PAC-MAN

15

The Game World

Most computer games are set in an imaginary world. This may be as small and simple as the room in which a card game is played, or it could be made up of hundreds of different locations in which many adventures take place.

Setting the scene

The game world includes the setting of the game. For example, a racing game or maze game might be set on a fantasy planet, in a jungle, a haunted house, or even under water. The game world provides the space through which a player's character travels. The game world's setting and background also add a certain mood to the game.

Big world

Some games have giant game worlds. World of Warcraft is a **massively multiplayer online game, or MMOG**. The original World of Warcraft game world had 1,400 different locations, which took 150 people more than four years to build. The finished game contained 5.5 million lines of computer code!

SIMULATION GAME WORLDS

In simulation games—those that simulate real-life places—the game world must be realistic and accurate. This can be a huge task in a big game like Microsoft's Flight Simulator X. This has 24,000 different airports, all modeled on real places.

Level up

Many games are divided up into sections known as levels. Players usually have to complete or reach a certain score on one level before moving on to the next. A good game gradually increases the difficulty as the player rises through the levels, providing them with new and tougher challenges.

TRUE STORY

Ruler of Games! A company called King created the smash hit puzzle game Candy Crush Saga in 2012. Since then it has continued to add levels for players to enjoy. By the start of 2017, the game boasted 2,845 levels!

STRETCH YOURSELF

On the Level

Design a level for a platform game. Decide on the setting for the game and create the background. Then add the platforms. Think of ways the character can move between platforms through the level. Ask yourself these questions:

☞ Is your game world going to be flat or three-dimensional (3-D)?

☞ What materials will each platform be made of?

☞ How many different routes around the level will there be?

☞ What obstacles and threats will you put in the character's way?

☞ How will you make the level that follows this level slightly more difficult?

Game Rules and Features

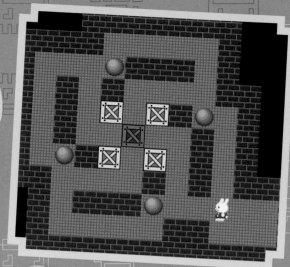

Every computer game has its own rules. The rules describe what players can and cannot do within the game. When you think up and design your first game, you have to create these rules. You also need to consider what other features will make your game fun and challenging.

Fair play

A good game sets challenges for players, but also gives them a chance to succeed. After all, if the game is too difficult, players probably won't come back for more! For example, in a maze game there must be a way out that the player can find. If a game includes enemies, there must be a way for the player's character to either avoid or defeat them.

COMPUTER Hero!

Thinking up and making computer game is certainly not just for boys. American programmer Lucy Bradshaw helped design and create The Sims life-simulation games, still one of the most successful game series ever made. In 2013, Bradshaw was named one of the ten most powerful women in gaming.

Lucy Bradshaw

Game over

Power-ups are little bonuses that can be gained during game-play. PAC-MAN was one of the first games to feature power-ups. PAC-MAN could gobble up one of four pellets on the screen. That gave PAC-MAN the ability, for a short time, to eat the ghosts chasing him, making them flee. Power-ups might be included to give a player extra energy, additional lives, or a burst of speed.

At some point, the game has to end. Game creators have to decide how a player can fail. Perhaps they run out of time or get caught by a monster. Many games give characters more than one life so they can carry on until all their lives are gone.

Fun Features
Some games have options for two players to take part. Others have a "level save" option, which means that a player does not have to go all the way back to the beginning if they fail on a later level. Other games contain hidden rewards called "Easter eggs." An Easter egg might be a joke, bonus lives, or tips on how to play the game.

TRUE STORY

Penguin Power!
An Easter egg inside the Pro Evolution Soccer 6 game allows players to turn their team of soccer players into giant penguins, or have their players ride Velociraptors!

Coding Games

Games are computer programs, and each program is made up of lines of computer code. These lines of code tell the computer to perform tasks such as move an object on the screen or display a message.

Learn a language

Lines of code are written in computer language. Common computer languages for major games include C and C++. Smaller games found on social media or as **apps** for **download** to smartphones are written in languages such as Java or Flash. Popular languages to learn for beginners are Scratch and Kodu.

SCRATCH

Scratch is a free computer language, designed for everyone from children to advanced programmers. It is made up of colorful blocks, which are the language's commands. These can be connected together to form a series of instructions called a script.

Scratch features moving objects called sprites. Each sprite can be designed to look like a person, a monster, or whatever object you like. Each sprite can be moved around the screen and instructed to react to other objects by a series of commands.

Getting it right

Creating code requires patience no matter which computer language is being used. Code has to be accurate and complete to make an object move correctly. You cannot just tell the computer to "move object A." You must specify how far and in which direction.

This simple Scratch script moves a sprite on a square-shaped path twice.

The script starts when GO! is clicked on the screen.

This block moves the sprite to a point on the screen.

This repeat block causes the sprite to turn and move eight times.

The sprite moves 200 steps in the direction it is facing. Each step is a tiny distance on the screen.

This block pauses movement for one second.

The sprite turns 90 degrees before moving again.

STRETCH YOURSELF

Scratch Puzzles

Looking at the script, can you solve these puzzles? (See answers on page 31.)

1. How would you make the sprite move around in a square shape three times?

2. Which two commands would you have to change to make the sprite move around the screen in a triangular shape twice?

when GO! clicked

glide 5 secs to x: 0 y: 100

repeat 8

move 200 steps

wait 1 secs

turn 90 degrees

Game engines

Major games are very complex. Hundreds of different objects need to move correctly and realistically. To help make this easier and more efficient to do, developers use a collection, or suite, of programs, referred to altogether as a game engine. These programs handle many tasks, including the basic movements, crashes, and bounces objects make in a game. Unity 3-D is an example of a game engine used by hundreds of games, from Angry Birds 2 and Kerbal Space Program to Temple Run and Pokémon GO.

Decision Time!

As a game is played, its program code is constantly making decisions. If you had to make so many decisions every second, your head would spin! Fortunately, computers are well suited to the task of dealing with a lot of information and instructions at the same time.

If...Then

If *Then*

Many decisions in game algorithms can be written in the form of an "IF...THEN" statement. This means IF a certain thing occurs, THEN the game will respond in a particular way. For example, if race cars must stay inside the edges of a track, an algorithm to keep them on the track might be written as:

1. Check position of car.
2. IF car touches left edge of track, THEN move car right 10 steps.
3. IF car touches right edge of track, THEN move car left 10 steps.

Algorithms

Algorithms are sets of step-by-step instructions that command a machine to perform a task or solve a problem. Game makers create algorithms to help plan out decisions in games before they write the code.

Crash!

Objects frequently touch or collide in action games. The code has to recognize a collision taking place and decide what happens next. The program first figures out what the character has touched, then decides what action should be taken according to the game's rules.

For example:
IF character touches candy,
THEN remove candy from screen and add 10 points to score.
or
IF character touches big monster,
THEN stop the game, display words "Game Over," and play sad music.

Go with the Flow

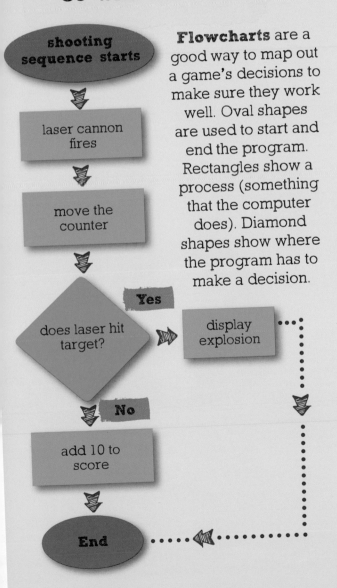

Flowcharts are a good way to map out a game's decisions to make sure they work well. Oval shapes are used to start and end the program. Rectangles show a process (something that the computer does). Diamond shapes show where the program has to make a decision.

STRETCH YOURSELF

Try Tynkering

Visit **www.tynker.com/hour-of-code/** to learn in a fun and interactive way how coding works. The Tynker programming area contains several simple games. You have to drag command blocks to an algorithm to make them work. The commands are based on Scratch. They will help you see how coding and decisions have to be made in games. Try out Scavenger Hunt, Candy Quest, and Dragon Dash first.

Controlling Games

All computer games need a way for the player to control the game. For example, players must be able to send instructions to the computer or console to shoot an alien spaceship, pick up a chess piece, or make their game character move or jump.

Game controllers

Game controllers are devices used to send instructions to the computer or console. Some games use a computer keyboard or mouse as the controller. Action games tend to be controlled by a joystick or a gamepad.

A joystick is gripped by the player who moves it in the direction he or she wants the game character to move. Gamepads sometimes have small joysticks or up/down and left/right arrows that do a similar job.

Smartphones and tablets have touchscreens. Games on these machines allow players to use their fingers to make moves and perform other commands by tapping or swiping the screen.

Custom controllers

Certain games require special controllers. For example, dance games often use a mat with special sensors inside. When a player's foot lands on a sensor's button, it sends a signal to the computer.

Car racing games can be extra fun if played with an acutal steering wheel, accelerator, and brake pedals, just like a real car.

TRUE STORY

Complex Controller. One of the most complicated game controllers ever made was built for a robot tank game called Steel Battalion. The controller featured two joysticks, three pedals operated by the player's feet, and 40 buttons!

In and Out

Work done by a computer, including a computer game, is performed in three stages. In the first stage, called input, a user, such as a game player, sends a command or information to the computer or game console. In the second stage, called processing, the machine works or acts on the input in some way. The final stage, called output, is the display of the computer's completed work, such as on-screen.

1. Input: The right arrow on a gamepad is pressed. This sends a signal to the computer.

2. Processing: The computer recognizes the input and checks to see if the character can move to the right in the game, or if there is something in its way.

3. Output: If the character cannot move, the computer might play a bumping sound. If there is enough space on the right, the character is shown moving across the screen.

Keeping Score

Part of the fun of many games is trying to beat your own score or the scores set by others. To do this, computer games need some sort of scoring system.

↓ Variables

Players gain points in many games by moving over or collecting certain objects. These objects are given a value in points. The game knows to add them to the player's score.

Points are often stored in a game's code in something called a **variable**. A variable is a small store of information that has a name. This can be accessed and changed by the game's code.

Coins n' Ghosts

In a simple coin-collecting game, players have to avoid ghosts. Written out, the code for the game's scoring might look like this:

IF player touches silver coin, THEN Score = Score + 5
(5 points are added to the score.)

IF player touches gold coin, THEN Score = Score + 10
(10 points are added to the score.)

IF player touches ghost, THEN Score = Score − 50
(50 points are taken away.)

☞ With 10 gold and 10 silver coins, what is the maximum score a player can obtain?

☞ With three ghosts, what is the worst possible score a player can obtain?
(See answers on page 31.)

High-score history

Early computer games could not keep track of high scores. It wasn't until the arrival of Space Invaders in 1978 that a high score could be saved in computer memory and displayed on the screen during the next game. This idea proved to be a smash hit, as players returned to the game again and again to try to beat the current high score.

Lives left

Many other variables are stored in games. For example, one might keep count of the number of lives a player's character has left. Algorithms in the game decide when a player loses a life, such as when a character falls into water or is caught by a monster. Sometimes, a variable stores the energy or health of a character. When it reaches zero, it removes one of the player's lives. This might be written as:

IF Energy = 0, THEN Lives = Lives −1

Coding high scores

Storing a high score requires its own variable, which can then be compared to the player's current score, like this:

**IF Score > High Score,
THEN High Score = Score**

Another variable will hold the player's name. Let's call it PN. This player's new score becomes the high score and is displayed beside the player's name:

Display PN, Display Score

TRUE STORY

Asteroids Champ! All the way back in 1982, Scott Safran set a new high score on the space game Asteroids at the age of 15. His tally of 41,336,440 points wasn't beaten by anyone else in the world for 28 years!

Testing and Launching

A game needs a lot of testing to make sure it doesn't contain **bugs**. Testing is carried out by the company making the game as well as by the game-playing community. When a game is almost ready to be launched, a **beta test** is usually done. Gamers try the game out and report any bugs or areas they feel could be improved.

Even when a game nears completion, the work is far from over. Coding all the action, movement, and features of a game can amount to tens or hundreds of thousands of lines of code. The game has to be fully tested before launch.

TRUE STORY

Bugs at Launch! Despite heavy testing, bugs can sometimes still make it through. In the football game Madden 15, one of the linebackers who should be 6.5 feet (2 meters) tall sometimes appears only 11 inches (30 centimeters) tall! In the Nintendo DS game Bubble Bobble Revolution, a bug stopped all players at level 30, not letting them play the game's 70 other levels.

Visitors to Games Week 2016, in Milan, Italy, are shown here trying out the new 3-D platform game, Skylanders Imaginators.

Gaining a Rating

In many countries, games have to be sent to an organization before launch to receive a rating. This rating advises customers what age the game is suitable for based on its content. In the United States, the Entertainment Software Rating Board (ESRB) awards ratings such as E (Everyone can play), E10+, T (Teens and above), and M (Mature audiences, age 17 and over).

Launch time

Major games are launched with a great deal of publicity and sometimes events or stunts. Games are either sold in physical form as program discs or memory cartridges, or they can be downloaded online. Early sales for a well-promoted game can be huge. In 2016, over five million copies of the PlayStation 4 game Final Fantasy XV were sold on the first day.

These people are playing Pokémon GO. Launched in July 2016, the game had been downloaded by over 100 million people by the end of that month.

Game over?

The work isn't over after a game is launched. Many coders and other staff might continue to work on the game. They fix any bugs that are found by customers. They do this by releasing files called fixes or patches that gamers can download for free to improve the performance of the game.

Sequels and Expansion Packs

If a game is popular, the team may start work on a follow-up or sequel, or produce what is called an expansion pack. This is an addition to the original game that adds extra content, such as new characters or more game levels for players to explore. World of Warcraft, for example, has been extended through six expansion packs.

Glossary

3-D Short for three-dimensional. A three-dimensional object on-screen appears to have depth as well as height and width.

algorithm A set of steps that are followed in order to solve a problem or perform a task

app A small computer program, such as a game that can be downloaded and used on mobile devices such as tablets and smartphones

assets All the things you can see in a game, including characters, vehicles, tools, weapons, and obstacles

avars Also known as hinge points, these are parts of an animation that can be altered to move part of the animated object

beta test A test on a game or other computer program to try to discover any faults before it is released

boss A powerful character in a game that a player must usually defeat at the end of a level

bug An error in the code of a computer game that produces an unexpected or unwanted result

console A machine solely used for playing games, such as an Xbox or PlayStation, which connects to a display monitor or TV screen

cutscene A scene in a game when gameplay stops (such as when a player completes a level) but movement on the screen continues

download To obtain a computer file or program such as a game from another computer, often by connecting to it over the Internet

flowchart A type of diagram that maps out the actions and decisions that occur within a program or part of a program

game controller The device gamers use to perform actions and commands in a game. Common controllers include a mouse, joystick, gamepad, and keyboard.

Internet A network that connects millions of computers all over the world

massively multiplayer online game (MMOG) A type of game in which individual players interact with a large number of other players in an imaginary world

memory Part of a computer or other digital device in which information can be stored for later use

pixels The dots of color that make up an image on a screen

porting Adapting a game so that it can be played on lots of different types of devices, such as smartphones, tablets, and handheld game consoles

power-up An object in a game that gives the player instant benefits, such as extra lives or more speed

simulation A game that tries to closely mimic or simulate real-world situations, such as flying an aircraft

storyboard A visual plan of all the scenes and shots in an animation

variable A place for storing information in a computer program, which can be changed by other parts of the program

Further Resources

Books

Programming Games and Animation (Kids Get Coding) by Heather Lyons and Alex Westgate (Lerner Classroom, 2017)

A Math Journey Through Computer Games (Go Figure!) by Hilary Koll and Steve Mills (Crabtree Publishing, 2016)

I'm a JavaScript Game Maker: The Basics by Max Wainewright (Crabtree Publishing, 2018)

I'm a JavaScript Game Maker: Advanced Coding by Max Wainewright (Crabtree Publishing, 2018)

I'm a Scratch Coder by Max Wainewright (Crabtree Publishing, 2018)

Websites

https://gridclub.com/activities/game-box
Play a game, then build your own with this animated activity. Works in web browsers Firefox, Safari, and Internet Explorer.

https://scratch.mit.edu/
This is the homepage of the Scratch programming language, which is great for learning to code simple computer games.

www.pbs.org/kcts/videogamerevolution/inside/how/
A website explaining how games are made, with some history on how computer games developed.

http://pixar-animation.weebly.com/three-dimensional-computer-animation.html
Watch behind-the-scenes videos of work at the movie animation company, Pixar.

Answers

page 7
Make History

a) 2009

b) 1994

c) 1981

d) 1972

e) 2006

f) 1983

g) 2005

h) 1989

page 21
Scratch Puzzles

1. Change "Repeat 8" to "Repeat 12".

2. Change "Repeat 8" to "Repeat 6" and change "Turn 90 degrees" to "Turn 60 degrees".

page 26
Coins n' Ghosts

150 (10 x 10 + 10 x 5)

−150 (3 x -50)

Index